ZOOM!

THE INVISIBLE WORLD OF...

BIRDS

Camilla de la Bédoyère

QED Publishing

Editor: Amanda Askew
Designer: Andrew Crowson
Picture Researcher: Maria Joannou

First published in the UK in 2011 by
QED Publishing
A Quarto Group company
226 City Road
London EC1V 2TT

www.qed-publishing.co.uk

A catalogue record for this book is available from the British Library.

ISBN 978 1 84835 567 5

Printed in China

▼ Without the aid of binoculars or a camera's zoom lens you could never expect to get this close to a great grey owl. Known as phantom or grey ghost owls, these nocturnal birds lead secretive lives in cold northern forests.

Picture credits
Corbis Micro Discovery 9tl;
FLPA Harri Taavetti 6b, 6-7t, Gerry Ellis/Minden Pictures 8b, Donald M. Jones 9tr, Photo Researchers 10c, Gerry Ellis/Minden Pictures 10b, John Hawkins 15b, Ingo Schulz/Imagebroker 19b, Wayne Hutchinson 21t, Frans Lanting 21b, John Zimmermann 22l, Jim Brandenburg/Minden Pictures 22r, Jurgen & Christine Sohns 22-23, Michael & Patricia Fogden/Minden Pictures 23tr, Frans Lanting 23b, S & D & K Maslowski 25bl, Richard Costin 27tr, Jurgen & Christine Sohns 28br, Harri Taavetti 28cl, Ingo Schulz/Imagebroker 29cl;
Nature Picture Library Jane Burton 4b, Philippe Clement 5b, Pete Cairns 7tr, Philippe Clement 7br, Charlie Hamilton James 9b, Rolf Nussbaumer 10-11t, Mike Potts 11tr, Wegner/ARCO 15tr, Wild Wonders of Europe/Varesvu 17tr, Wild Wonders of Europe/Widstrand 17b, Jane Burton 20b (stage 2), 21cl, Pete Cairns 24l, Andy Rouse 27b, Charlie Hamilton James 28t, Wild Wonders of Europe/Widstrand 28bl, Rolf Nussbaumer 29tr, Jane Burton 29cr, Andy Rouse 29bl, Rolf Nussbaumer 30, Steve Knell 32;
Photolibrary Oxford Scientific/Lewis Phillips 7bl, Phototake Science 12b, Juniors Bildarchiv 14c, Phototake Science 14b, Doug Allan 24b, Tony Tilford 25t, Doug Allan 26b, Tony Tilford 29br;
Photoshot NHPA/Nick Garbutt 11b;
Science Photo Library Steve Gschmeissner 13tl, Herve Conge, ISM 20b (stage 1), Kenneth H Thomas 21cr;
Shutterstock Blacqbook 4t, Frog-traveller 5t, Iv Nikolny 8t, Chris Pole 12l, MustafaNC 13tr, Nicholas Moore 13b, Joanne Harris and Daniel Bubnich 14-15, Eduardo Rivero 16l, Bernd Schmidt 16b, Dhoxax 17tl, Christian Musat 18c, Bernd Schmidt 18b, Stephen Chung 18-19, Frog-traveller 19t, Valentina_G 20t, Saied Shahin Kiya 20b (stage 3), Xavier Marchant 25br, Chris Alcock 26t, Martin Pateman 26-27, Iv Nikolny 28cr, Eduardo Rivero 29tl
Front and back cover Nature Picture Library

Words in **bold** can be found in the Glossary on page 30.

CONTENTS

ZOOM INTO...

...the world of birds and begin a journey that takes you high into the skies, and up to the highest treetops, where nests balance unsafely. When these agile dancers of the air swoop and soar, they make a beautiful sight. But when you zoom up close, you will discover the secrets of flight, feathers and new life.

Zoom inside

Look at a feather through a microscope and you will notice that it appears bigger than in real life, and you will see details you never saw before. Zoom close to a bird using a pair of **binoculars**, and you will be able to watch these shy animals in action: feeding, flying and **preening**. Microscopes and binoculars use lenses to magnify images, making them appear larger, or closer.

Almost real

Birds with the ACTUAL SIZE icons are shown at their real-life size, as though they're flying across the page! Comparing the bird to a paperclip really helps you to understand its size.

ACTUAL SIZE

Macro photography

This is the art of taking pictures of small things in close-up. Using these, and other techniques, photographers and scientists have helped us to uncover a world we never knew existed, and given us a bird's eye view.

ZOOM x2

Try it

WHAT IS IT? photographs let you use your new investigative skills to guess what the bird or bird feature might be. Then just turn over the page to find out that IT IS…

WHAt iS it?

ZOOM x8

SILENT BUT DEADLY

The feathers on an owl's face help to focus sound towards its ears.

Owl

Owls are the silent hunters of the night. Under cover of darkness, they swoop through the forest, searching for small animals to eat. With superb eyesight, they can spot the smallest movement and quietly move in for the kill.

Eyes to the front
While most birds have eyes on the sides of their head, owls have eyes that face forwards. Forward-facing eyes are better for focusing on prey, to judge both distance and the speed of movement.

ACTUAL SIZE

These owls fly with soft, slow wingbeats, often close to the ground.

Softly, softly

*Owls have soft **downy** feathers on their body and feet. These help to muffle the noise of their wings in flight, and means they can approach their prey in silence. Feathers around their ears help direct sound straight into the ear canal.*

The bill is usually hooked and sharp for tearing at meat.

ACTUAL SIZE

Feathers are often coloured to provide **camouflage**.

FACTOID

Eurasian eagle owls are huge, with a wingspan of 2 metres. They can attack and kill foxes, small deer and other large owls.

It is...

an owl pellet. Owls can't digest all of the bones, claws, fur and teeth they swallow. These hard bits are collected in part of the bird's stomach, then brought up and coughed out of the mouth as a pellet.

VITAL STATISTICS

Common name	Eurasian eagle owl
Latin name	*Bupo bupo*
Size	58–70 cm in length
Habitat	Forests, grasslands and deserts
Special feature	Calls "ouho-oohu-oohu"

HIGH FLIERS

Even with a pair of binoculars in your hands, it is hard to imagine how birds fly. Scientists had to zoom in close, and look at how birds' bodies are built, to understand the phenomenon of flight. It is all to do with feathers, wing shape and power.

Why fly?

There are only three types of animals that can truly fly – insects, bats and birds. Flight takes lots of energy, and a specially adapted body, but there are advantages to a life in the air. An animal that flies can explore new areas to live or feed, escape predators and find mates.

▲ A hungry African fish eagle soars above water, looking for fish.

WHAT is it?

ZOOM x7

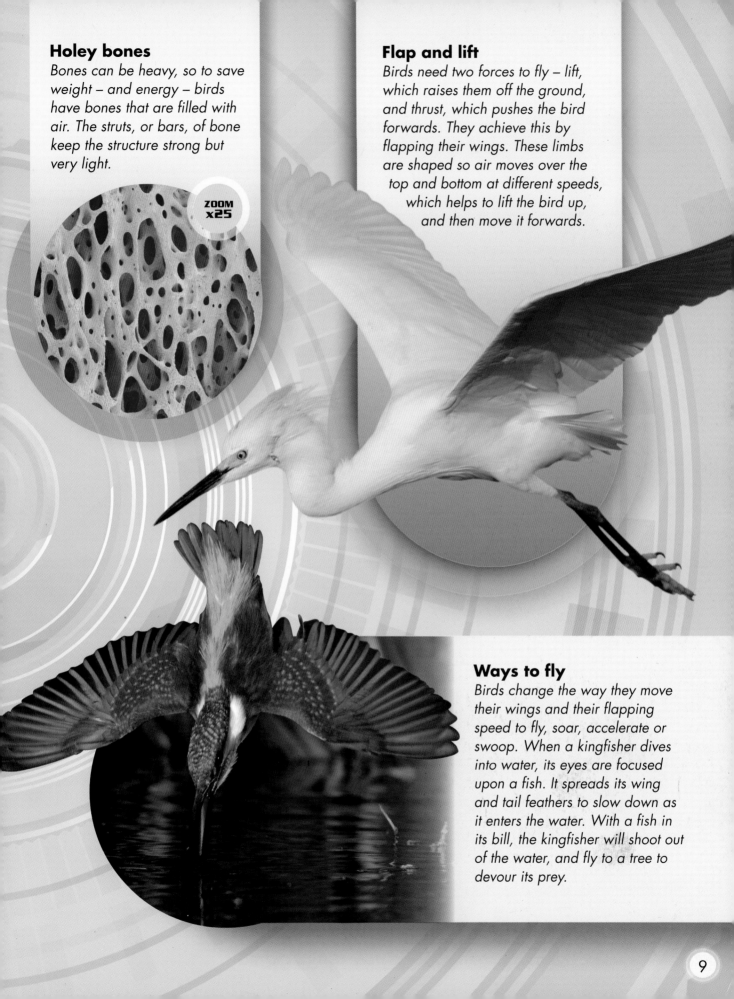

Holey bones

Bones can be heavy, so to save weight – and energy – birds have bones that are filled with air. The struts, or bars, of bone keep the structure strong but very light.

ZOOM x25

Flap and lift

Birds need two forces to fly – lift, which raises them off the ground, and thrust, which pushes the bird forwards. They achieve this by flapping their wings. These limbs are shaped so air moves over the top and bottom at different speeds, which helps to lift the bird up, and then move it forwards.

Ways to fly

Birds change the way they move their wings and their flapping speed to fly, soar, accelerate or swoop. When a kingfisher dives into water, its eyes are focused upon a fish. It spreads its wing and tail feathers to slow down as it enters the water. With a fish in its bill, the kingfisher will shoot out of the water, and fly to a tree to devour its prey.

SPEEDY WINGS

Little hummingbirds are like flying gems of the forest. They zip and dart through the air, visiting up to 2000 **tropical** flowers a day to feed at lightning speed. This way of life is so exhausting that hummingbirds spend most of their time asleep or resting!

Beating its wings 50 times every single minute enables the bird to hover, but it burns energy fast.

Air acrobats

These birds can feed at flowers by hovering – flying while staying in one place. Hummingbirds achieve this incredible feat by moving their wings in a figure-of-eight rather than flapping them up and down.

ACTUAL SIZE

It is...

a hummingbird nest. These little birds lay the smallest eggs, with some no bigger than a pea. The nests and eggs of some hummingbirds are so small and well hidden that they have never been found.

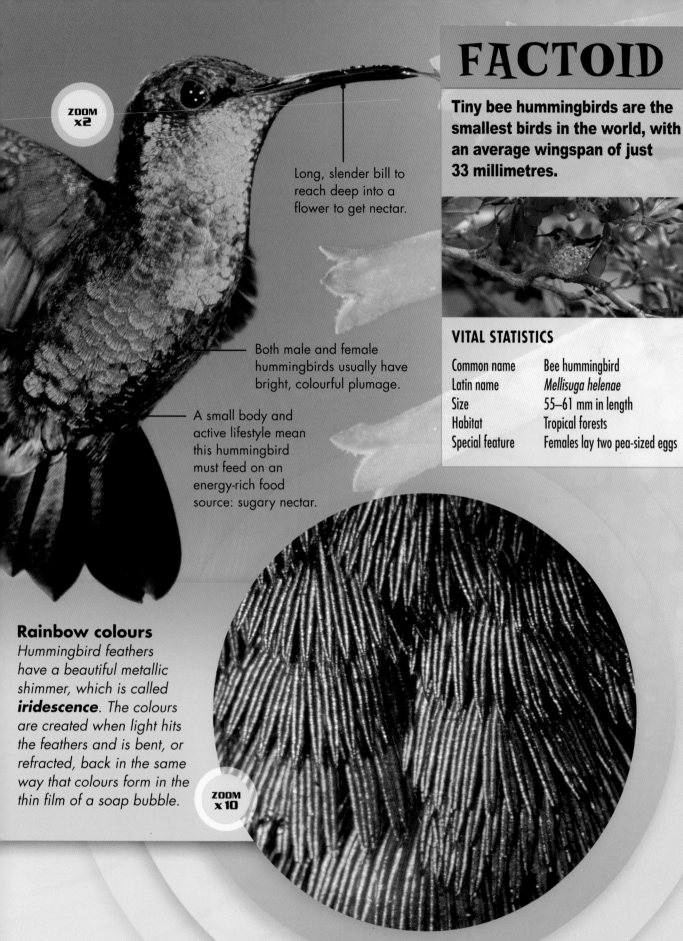

Long, slender bill to reach deep into a flower to get nectar.

Both male and female hummingbirds usually have bright, colourful plumage.

A small body and active lifestyle mean this hummingbird must feed on an energy-rich food source: sugary nectar.

FACTOID

Tiny bee hummingbirds are the smallest birds in the world, with an average wingspan of just 33 millimetres.

VITAL STATISTICS

Common name	Bee hummingbird
Latin name	*Mellisuga helenae*
Size	55–61 mm in length
Habitat	Tropical forests
Special feature	Females lay two pea-sized eggs

Rainbow colours

Hummingbird feathers have a beautiful metallic shimmer, which is called **iridescence**. *The colours are created when light hits the feathers and is bent, or refracted, back in the same way that colours form in the thin film of a soap bubble.*

ZOOM
x 10

FINE FEATHERS

Feathers are super structures that have extraordinary properties. They keep birds dry, warm or cool – and are essential for flight. Feathers are made of **keratin**, which is the same protein you have in your nails and hair.

◄ Male and female grey crowned cranes wear splendid **crests** of stiff, gold feathers.

ACTUAL SIZE

Pretty plumage

A bird's feathers are called its plumage and the colours are a balance between camouflage and attention-seeking. Birds that need to hide from predators often have dull, brown plumage. Others – often male birds – like to show off with fine feathers, bold colours and impressive crests or tails.

ZOOM
x 120

WHAT
IS IT?

Zoom a plume

A powerful microscope, called a scanning electron microscope, reveals the incredible structure of a penguin's feather. Orange **barbs** fan out from a central shaft, or **rachis**. Each barb has many tiny hooked filaments, called **barbules**. They hook together, trapping air to keep the bird warm, and helping to make its plumage waterproof.

ZOOM
x100

Feather types

A bird's large, stiff feathers are mostly used for flight, and are found on its wings and tail. Contour feathers, like this one, grow over the bird's body. The barbs overlap, and help to give a bird its streamlined shape. Soft, downy **plumes** near the base of the feather's rachis trap air and insulate the body (keep it warm by preventing the bird's body heat from escaping).

ZOOM
x3

Fit for flight

Flight feathers are called ramiges. Primary flight feathers, like these, grow on the wingtips and can be spread out to give the wing a large surface area. A bird can fan its ramiges out, or twist them, to control the direction and speed of flight. Like ramiges, a bird's tail feathers are stiff and can be moved. By dipping and spreading its tail feathers, a bird can rapidly slow down to avoid a crash-landing.

FABULOUS FINCH

Gouldian finches have such colourful feathers, they look as if they have been dipped in paint. These birds live only in parts of northern Australia, where they were once common. Now Gouldian finches are rare and fewer than 250 live in the wild.

Stout, strong bill for cracking open seeds.

Black, red or orange-yellow face

Drab chicks

Gouldian finches may stay with the same mate for life. The chicks have a drab plumage compared to their parents. Until they can fly the nest, the chicks are vulnerable to predators. Flashy feathers would be like wearing an "Eat me" sign!

ACTUAL SIZE

Gouldian finch

ZOOM x2

It is...

a bird feather louse, a type of **parasite**, nestled between feather barbs. Some bird parasites eat feathers; others suck blood. Gouldian finches suffer from burrowing mite parasites, which feed on their skin.

Brightly coloured plumage

Males have longer tails than females.

Sixty years ago, there were millions of Gouldian finches. They are so rare because many have been captured to be kept in cages, and their forest habitat has been destroyed.

VITAL STATISTICS

Common name	Gouldian finch
Latin name	*Erythrura gouldiae*
Size	13 cm in length
Habitat	Grasslands and forests
Special feature	Incredible colours

Handsome hawfinch
The plumage of this male hawfinch will impress any females nearby. These finches live in cooler places than Gouldian finches, and balance the need for fine feathers with an ability to hide from predators in dense woodlands. Their tough bills can break open olive and cherry stones.

ZOOM
x2

IT FITS THE BILL

When you look closely at a bird, pay particular attention to the shape and size of its bill. This tough, toothless mouth can tell you more about how the bird lives its life than any other body part. A bill grows from a bird's skull, and it keeps growing throughout a bird's life. It is constantly worn away, so it doesn't get any bigger in an adult bird.

ACTUAL SIZE

Big mouth
Toucans have huge, colourful bills. These tropical birds don't need big bills for their diet of fruit and insects, so why carry around such big mouths? No one knows, although a big bill may work like a giant air-conditioning unit, helping the birds to stay cool.

WHAT IS it?

ZOOM x4

Small but strong

Cone-shaped bills are particularly strong near the base. They are the perfect shape for tackling hard nuts, and getting through a tough skin and into the soft flesh of a fruit. This greenfinch uses its cone-shaped bill to crack open sunflower seeds.

Keeping a safe distance

Birds that eat insects have tweezer-like bills. The bills are often long, to keep a bird safe from stings or bites. Bee-eaters grab their prey in their bills, and hit them against a branch until they have released their sting.

Table manners

Birds of prey, such as this white-tailed eagle, tear at meat. These huge birds **scavenge**, which means they feed on dying or dead animals. A long bill helps to keep bacteria and blood away from their feathers, eyes and nostrils.

BRILLIANT BIRDS

African grey parrots are super smart birds. In fact, they are so clever, some people think that they are as intelligent as whales, apes and even young children! Parrots are noisy, colourful birds that live in large groups, or **colonies**.

Bare skin around yellow eye

Sharp, hooked bill

Unusual feeding

Parrots, such as this scarlet macaw, use their feet like hands, grabbing hold of food to bring it up to their mouth. Blue hyacinth macaws eat tough palm nuts. They often pick nuts out of cow dung because they are easier to eat after they have been through a cow's digestive system!

ACTUAL SIZE

It is...

a hill mynah. These glossy birds are famous for their ability to mimic, or copy, human voices. Parrots not only mimic; they can learn the meaning of some words.

Light fantastic

The colours of parrot feathers are unique, and are created in a way shared by no other birds. Parrot feathers scatter light, and contain unusual pigments (substances that create colour) to produce vivid blues, greens and reds.

ACTUAL SIZE

Grey feathers
with white edges

Grey parrot

Adults are not as colourful as many other parrots, but they do have cherry-red tail feathers.

FACTOID

Members of the parrot family can live long lives – up to 80 years. However, this group of birds is threatened with extinction.

VITAL STATISTICS

Common name	African grey parrot
Latin name	*Psittacus erithacus*
Size	33 cm in length
Habitat	Lowland tropical forest
Special feature	Talkative

THE MIRACLE OF AN EGG

Female birds lay eggs, and most parent birds look after their chicks as they grow. If you could look inside an egg, and watch a chick develop, you would observe one of nature's most incredible events.

ACTUAL SIZE

◀ It took about 21 days for this baby chicken to develop inside its egg. Smaller birds, such as sparrows, can hatch in less than two weeks.

A chick's life cycle

1 ***Membranes*** *keep liquids in the egg, and allow gases to pass through the shell. The yellow yolk contains food for the growing chick.*

2 *The shell gets thinner as the chick grows. The calcium it contains is used to build the chick's skeleton.*
Egg white (albumen) protects the chick, and provides food.

3 *Chicks have a small 'tooth' on their bill, which they use to crack open the shell.*

4 *A newly hatched chick has damp feathers, but they soon dry to become soft and fluffy.*

Grow zone

Eggs contain all the goodness a growing chick will need before it hatches. However, the chicks need to be kept warm to develop. This means the parents have to sit on the eggs – it is a process called incubation.

ACTUAL SIZE

Hens lay eggs

All female birds are called hens, not just those of chickens. The eggs are developing inside the body even before the hens mate with the male birds. The male birds fertilize the eggs during mating.

Feed me!

Chicks can open their large mouths extra wide. They rely on their parents to bring food to them while they grow. When they are ready to fly, they are called fledglings.

ZOOM x4

WHAT iS it?

ACTUAL SIZE

BUILDING MARVELS

Weavers are the best builders in the bird world. They build the most extraordinary nests. Look closely, and you will see that they don't just pile bits of plants on top of each other – they actually weave them together to create an elaborate and strong fortress.

Grasses or reeds are woven together to create the nest walls.

ZOOM
x2

Mud and spit
Swallows build their nests with mud and spit then line it with soft straw and feathers. Tucked away in their cup-shaped nest, these barn swallow chicks can feed and grow, while staying out of danger from predators.

FACTOID

Cape weavers sometimes build nests that hang from branches above water, where few predators can reach them. But if the water level rises, the nest will flood and the chicks will drown.

VITAL STATISTICS

Common name	Cape weaver
Latin name	*Ploceus capensis*
Size	18 cm in length
Habitat	Woodlands
Special feature	Superb nest builders

The nest entrance is usually a tunnel.

Watch me!
Male satin bowerbirds decorate their bowers with any blue or yellow objects they can find. The bower is like a stage, where the males dance and display for females.

The male builds the nest, then sings and dances to entice females to inspect his handiwork.

Weaver bird

It is...

an Emperor penguin chick. There are no nest-building materials in its Antarctic home, so the parents hold the egg, and then the chick, on their feet to keep it warm.

The nest is built between two supports, such as branches or thick grass stems.

PERCH, WALK AND WADE

You can tell a lot about a bird by looking at its feet. Just as a close-up view of a bird's bill will give you clues about its diet, zooming in on a bird's lower limbs will tell you something about where, and how, it lives.

◄ A close-up of a white-tailed eagle as it swoops in for the kill reveals the power of this mighty predator.

Non-slip feet

*Birds of prey grab hold of squirming creatures, so they need strong, clawed **talons** to grip tightly. White-tailed eagles pluck slippery fish out of water but they are also equipped to hunt mammals and other birds, and to scavenge.*

x100 Zoom

WHAT IS IT?

ZOOM x2

ACTUAL SIZE

Waterbirds
Birds, such as coots, that wade through shallow water looking for small animals to eat often have long slender legs. Their feet have long toes that are spread far apart, to stop the bird from sinking into mud. Swimming birds, such as ducks and penguins, have webbed feet. Webbing helps them to move through water with speed and power.

ZOOM x2

Sleep tight
Perching birds, or passerines, have three toes pointing forwards on each foot, and one toe pointing behind. This arrangement means a passerine can grip tightly on to a branch, even when it is asleep.

Big kickers
Ostriches are huge birds that can run at speeds of 70 kilometres an hour, but cannot fly. They have just two large, fat toes on each foot and are able to kick with enough force to kill a lion.

HUNTERS BY THE SEA

Puffins are one of the world's strangest-looking birds. They have been called 'sea parrots' and 'clowns of the ocean' because of their comical face and coloured bill. These striking seabirds are not great fliers, but their swimming and hunting skills are awesome.

Grey or white face

Strong, conical bill

Puffin

Brightly coloured bill in summer – with blue, red and yellow parts

ZOOM x2

All at sea

Puffins are fearless swimmers in the open oceans, paddling with their large orange webbed feet. They can dive deep below the surface, as far as 20 metres, in pursuit of prey and can stay there for up to 30 seconds at a time.

It is...

the egg of a guillemot. These seabirds lay their eggs directly on to a bare cliff edge, with no nest to protect them. The unusual shape of the egg prevents it from rolling off.

Unusual red and black eye markings

During the breeding season, a parent puffin may have to carry its hoard of food up to 50 kilometres, back to the nest and hungry chicks.

VITAL STATISTICS

Common name	Atlantic puffin
Latin name	*Fratercula arctica*
Size	27–30 cm in length
Habitat	Sea cliffs and open seas
Special feature	Feed in large groups called rafts

A white breast and a black body

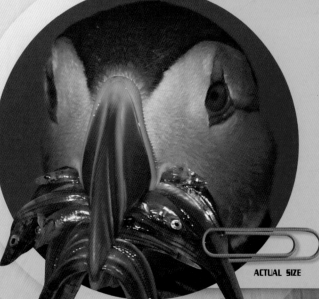

ACTUAL SIZE

Ferrying fish
Once a puffin has reached its prey – usually small fish – it can catch and hold several at a time. It does this by pushing a fish up with its tongue, onto spikes on the roof of its mouth. It can then safely open its mouth to catch more.

Use your eyes to study these zooms of birds that appear throughout the book. Can you recognize any of them just by looking at them? Are there any clues, such as colour, body parts or shape, that help you work out where you've seen these images before?

1 *I look like I've been dipped in paint.*

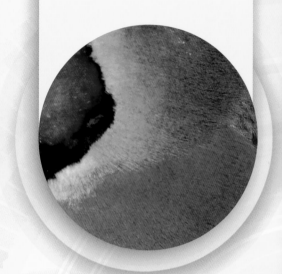

2 *Shhh, I've got my eyes on you. I'm a silent hunter, so you won't hear me coming.*

3 *I spread my enormous wings and swoop over water.*

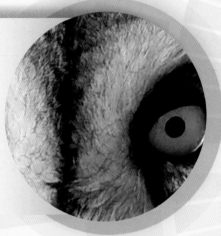

4 *I have brown plumage, but a white tail.*

5 *What yellow bird has been busy weaving this nest?*

6 Two can see better than one, but one can see you!

7 I fly so fast I'm just a beautiful blue blur.

9 Welcome to the world, baby bird!

8 I am smart, I can talk and I am handsome, too.

11 Who wants neat feet when you are wading through mud? I like my big feet, but who am I?

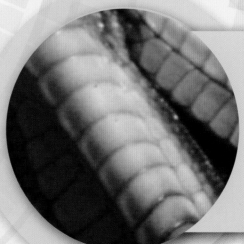

10 They say I look like a clown or a parrot. Do you agree?

Answers: 1. p14–15 2. p6–7 3. p8 4. p17 5. p23 6. p16 7. p11 8. p18 9. p20 10. p26–27 11. p25

GLOSSARY

Barb A hair-like thread that grows from a feather's main shaft.

Barbule A tiny thread that grows from a barb.

Binoculars An instrument with lenses that is used for seeing objects that are far away.

Camouflage Colours or patterns that help an animal to stay hidden from view.

Colony A group of animals that live closely together.

Crest Many birds have decorative feathers on their head, which are known as crests. They may be used to impress mates.

Downy Soft, fine and fluffy. Downy feathers are ideal for keeping a bird warm.

Iridescence Colours that seem to change when they are seen from different angles are described as iridescent.

Keratin A tough substance that is used in nature to make skin, nails, hair, scales, hooves and feathers.

Membrane A thin layer, like a sheet, that separates the inside parts of an animal's body or makes a lining around organs.

Parasite A living thing that survives by feeding from, or living in, another animal or plant, known as a 'host'. Parasites always harm the host.

Plume This is another word for a feather, especially one that is colourful or downy.

Preening The way a bird cleans and straightens its feathers.

Rachis The central shaft of a feather.

Scavenge A method of feeding that involves finding and eating any available food, including animals that have died naturally.

Talons A bird of prey's powerful, clawed feet.

Tropical The 'tropics' are a region of the Earth near the Equator, between the Tropic of Cancer and the Tropic of Capricorn. Tropical areas have days and nights of similar length, and have hot climates.

Wingspan The measurement across both of a bird's outstretched wings. The measurement is taken from tip to tip.

INDEX

NOTES FOR PARENTS AND TEACHERS

Photography and the use of binoculars are two ways that the physics of light and lenses can be applied to our everyday lives. Use the Internet* to find diagrams that show how lenses bend (refract) light that goes through them. Look at diagrams that show both convex and concave lenses, to discover how the shape of the lens changes the effect. Together, you can work out which of these two types of lens is used in binoculars and microscopes. Use the Internet to explore the role of lenses in the human eye, and how corrective lenses in spectacles are used to improve eyesight.

On a sunny day, you can demonstrate the focusing power of a lens. Hold a magnifying lens just above a piece of paper that is laid out in sunshine. Angle the lens until the light is focused on the paper, as a small bright dot. As it heats, the paper will smoke and burn.

It is easy to make a water lens that shows how even a simple lens can magnify images. Lay a piece of clingfilm or other transparent plastic over a piece of newspaper text. Use a syringe or a teaspoon to place a single drop of water on the plastic. You will notice that the text beneath the water drop is magnified. Find out what happens when you make the drop bigger, or smaller.

Zoom into the world of birds together, with a pair of binoculars and an identification book. This simple activity helps children learn the rewards of sitting quietly and observing. Record the species you identify and sketch or photograph them. Teach the child to look for specific identifiers, such as size, colour, tail length and birdsong. Further research can delve into a species' mating, migrating and breeding patterns, its preferred food and habitat.

Many naturalists discover a love of wildlife as children, simply by observing animals and taking notes about their behaviour. Teach children to respect the wildlife around them, and to avoid disturbing animals' habitats. Explain to them that they must not approach or investigate any active nest, as the parent birds may abandon their eggs or chicks.

*The publishers cannot accept any liability for the content of Internet websites, including third-party websites.